University College Birmingham

UCB

THE GOUDE TOUCH

THE GOUDE TOUCH

A TEN YEAR CAMPAIGN FOR GALERIES LAFAYETTE

Jean-Paul Goude
With an introduction by Patrick Mauriès

Thames & Hudson

IN THE BEGINNING

Sketch for generic image, 2001.

STORE STORIES

Where does this story begin?

Is it with the 'little box', with just two or three counters, that Alphonse Kahn opened in January 1894, on the corner of the rue Lafayette and the rue de la Chaussée-d'Antin, to sell frills and flounces, trinkets and ribbons, violets and haberdashery?

Or should we start with the office of one of his distant heirs, third in the unusual line of sons-in-law who arrived to run the business, an heir who decided, when he took over in 1998, that it was time to reinvent the brand and the image of this place?

Perhaps we should start with the advertising agency whose creatives strive to make these great institutional machines stand out from each other, working on targeted campaigns adapted to the exact needs of each client?

Or in the notebooks and sketchpads in which Jean-Paul Goude collects tiny drawings and multi-layered collages that become his treasure chest, a whole set of forms for his towering monuments?

Perhaps we should go all the way back to the little shops like Le Petit Dunkerque, the French draper's stores of the 18th century – or perhaps a less elitist and therefore more fitting choice would be the general stores, like Mr Johnson's 'universal shop' in Elizabeth Gaskell's *Cranford* (1853), whose proprietor lived above his premises and 'ranged the trades from grocer and cheesemonger to man-milliner, as occasion required'.

Alison Adburgham (*Shops and Shopping 1800–1914*, London, 1964) dates the appearance of this new mode of distribution and sale of goods to 1815, as an indirect consequence of the Industrial Revolution and the new methods of production that followed. (The invention of the Jacquard loom and machine-made lace date from the same period; as another reference point, the move from handmade to mass-produced shoes occurred between 1850 and 1870.)

Retailers began to bring their goods together in a single space that was more reminiscent of an Eastern bazaar (the model that Alphonse Kahn and Théophile Bader followed in their early years) than a modern store. The Galerie de Boufflers on the Grands-Boulevards, destroyed by a fire on 26 March 1829, included a menagerie and a *salon de curiosités*; at the Palais Bonne Nouvelle and the Bazar de l'Industrie, explains Paul Jarry (*Les magasins de nouveauté*, Paris, 1948), 'every new invention is an opportunity to open a new department' within a space that was by definition impossible to extend, and therefore increasingly chaotic; the Pantechnicon bazaar that opened in London in the 1830s offered a range of goods that rivalled the impossible Chinese encyclopedia described by Jorge Luis Borges.

However diverse in location and surroundings, these places shared a common determining factor: they were completely different from the basic and enclosed boutiques on the street. One striking characteristic was light: Balzac was quick to praise the Le Persan store on rue de Richelieu, on the corner of rue de la Bourse, which was among the first in France to have large windows to bring light into the interior as well as allowing the goods to be displayed. A second feature was the range of goods on sale: 'despite the size of the shop,' says one of the first in-store publications in 1845, 'the eye can take in at once all the manufactured riches that it holds; light falls in profusion.' (Jarry 1948, p. 143; according to Adburgham, the first examples of store advertisements aimed at ladies began to appear in the press in 1813.) A third quality was the democratization of goods: 'to satisfy at the best possible price the taste for elegance and comfort unknown to previous generations' was how Georges Michel summed up the mission of these new emporiums in the *Revue des deux mondes* ('Défense et illustration des grands magasins', 1892).

Here then are the basic elements of a typology. To these, we could add a characteristic that is mentioned in Balzac's *The Rise and Fall of César Birotteau*: the fictional draper's shop known as Le Petit Matelot is decked with 'painted signs, floating banners, show-cases filled with swinging shawls, cravats arranged like houses of cards, and a thousand other commercial seductions, such as fixed prices, fillets of suspended objects, placards, illusions and optical effects carried to such a degree of perfection that a shop-front has now become a commercial poem.' This is an early example of the transformation of retail into fantasy that fascinated Walter Benjamin, and Jean-Paul Goude's images are simply a continuation of this transformation by other means, its distant and sophisticated heirs.

The 'commercial poem' set a new rhythm, and new Parisian cathedrals of commerce were raised at a steady pace as the 19th century wore on: À la Belle Jardinière opened on 25 October 1824, Les Trois Quartiers in 1829, the Magasins du Louvre on 9 July 1855, the Bazar de l'Hôtel de Ville five years later, Le Printemps on 11 March 1855, and finally La Samaritaine in 1870.

Within this commercial landscape, Alphonse Kahn's 'little box' had no choice but to expand: in partnership with his cousin Théophile Bader (to whom he soon entrusted control of the business), Kahn enlarged the store, two years after its opening, by moving along the rue Lafayette, then annexed new premises on the rue de la Chaussée-d'Antin in 1898, before doubling the space by taking over 38–40 Boulevard Haussmann between 1900 and 1905.

The store found its definitive face in 1912 through the architectural talents of Georges Chedanne and later Ferdinand Chanut, with the 33-metre-high dome that stands out on the Paris skyline and the chamfered façade that forms its figurehead on the street.

This architectural transformation is clearly significant: beneath the light that shines down from above and envelops the goods on display, we move from the fantasy of the Oriental bazaar (a potent concept when the department store was born) to that of the ocean liner, a symbol of modernity, dynamism and spatial unity, a dynamism that was reinforced by the arrival of Théophile Bader's sons-in-law as directors, Raoul Meyer (in 1919) and Max Heilbronn (in 1926), then Étienne Moulin (in 1946) and Georges Meyer (in 1964), the precursors of the current 'president'.

ADVERTISING STORIES

The time has come to examine some of the variables that play a part in Jean-Paul Goude's campaigns: the dialectical tension between the 'products' and the 'brand', the degree to which the former are neutralized or subsumed by the latter, and the affirmation of the store's identity. The story of the department store seems to be made up of a systolic and diastolic movement between the absorption of products by their brand, the insertion of 'little boxes' in the form of departments and concessions within the whole, and their assertion and relative autonomy.

From the beginning, the history and identity of the Galeries Lafayette have been marked by the desire for integration of, and identification with, the brand. As many specialist works note, Théophile Bader was the first to design and manufacture his own clothing lines – sold under the charmingly old-fashioned name of 'Eversmart' – at a time when other stores, following the old example of the draper's shop, were content to distribute goods that they did not manufacture (we can see how this model has changed today, with the transformation of the very nature of the department store and its types).

When Philippe Houzé became the head of Galeries Lafayette after the death of Georges Meyer in 1998, he had a similar wish, a century after Bader, to affirm the store's identity, but in a completely different way: it was less about selling products, even store-branded ones, than selling a symbolic set of values (including humour, dynamism, energy and a kind of Parisian mythology, among other things), and moving in its own terms towards true brand status.

In some sense, this means a reversal of strategy or outlook in the face of what had been until that point the discreet – and distinctly Swiss – house style (most of the designers involved came from Zurich). From the 1950s onwards, driven by Jean and Jacques Adnet (the latter responsible for a considerable body of work within the field of decorative art), the image of the Galeries had remained remarkably coherent. This image was cast in a new light by the arrival of Jean Widmer in 1959: not for nothing was Widmer a pupil and heir of Johannes Itten, one of the most influential members of the Bauhaus. When he left the Galeries Lafayette in 1961 to become artistic director of *Jardin des Modes*, Peter Knapp, a young man fresh from the Zurich School of Art, took over. Open spaces, dynamic layouts, a taste for simple shapes and styles, and strong, expressive typography in a central role: these became the elements of an immediately recognizable lexicon, one that the young designer would also use in his later work for *Elle* magazine. It was Knapp who was responsible for goods being displayed flat, sufficient in themselves, freed from the human figure, an assumed style that became a symbol of the consumerist modernity of the store, provider of an ever-changing range of products. This choice was in its turn reversed by Goude through his reintroduction of the mannequin, not as a simple clothes horse but as an element in a story in which an imaginary cast of characters works to serve the brand, becoming its physical embodiment and transforming it into fiction.

'La mode est là' – 'Fashion is here' – was for many years the house's slogan, created by Bruno Sutter, one of the most influential advertising designers in the history of the Galeries, and this was the old and triumphant type of claim that was needed. But while Sutter, in collaboration with Georges Meyer, had chosen to attach to the products not only a slogan but a logo – undoubtedly a strong and very identifiable sign, but a simple logo nonetheless – in Houzé's view it was necessary to recreate not simply the image but the imaginative world of the brand.

If, as specialists say, strategy can be analysed in terms of needs, the direction chosen was a response to the needs of the market, and to the changes that were affecting the very nature and definition of the department store, changes that were by no means unique to France, although they did taken their own particular form there. In a sector which has been marked by increasing polarization between mass-market discount stores on one hand and specialist stores (devoted to culture, electronics or fashion alone, for example) on the other hand, the traditional department store, historically designed to sell a complete and multifaceted range of goods, finds itself on difficult ground, obliged to play on both fields without really fitting into either. Although from the 1930s to the 1950s it was almost dominant from a commercial point of view, by the late 20th century it represented merely a small percentage of sales, and this percentage decreased even further as a result of new competition from online stores.

With the rise in discount stores from the 1970s on, the Galeries had no choice but to aim higher, seeking out new international markets among others, perhaps to the detriment of their mass-market appeal, which had resulted in the creation of the annual '3J' ('*3 jours*', or 3 days) sale event in the 1960s. In 1985, Georges Meyer set up a 'street of fashion', bringing together different designers within the store; in the same spirit, under Philippe Houzé, the Galeries sought out brands and designers that would boost their own lines and offer different options for different lifestyles. Therefore, of the three floors of the main store, one is devoted to very contemporary, creative and cutting-edge fashion, another to a more mainstream and accessible range, and the last to designer ready-to-wear and couture. An equally diverse range of men's fashion occupies its own space, while Lafayette Maison, located on the other side of the Boulevard Haussmann, concentrates on lifestyle and homeware.

Of course, it was not only French department stores that found themselves obliged to move with the times. On the other side of the Channel, Selfridges was transformed under chief executive Vittorio Radice to fit the demands of modern living and appeal to a younger generation of shoppers, while big US stores such as Barneys, Bloomingdale's and Macy's have also undergone similar reinventions.

*

Strategic reinvention of this kind requires flexible and innovative tactics; so perhaps we can imagine the relative disappointment of the store's new chief at the fairly traditional proposals submitted by ad agencies that had previously worked with the Galeries or with other large institutions. Affirming the spirit of a brand while at the same time emphasizing a desire for mobility and lightness means to some extent a return to another former slogan of the store, this time by Marcel Bleustein-Blanchet: '*Il se passe toujours quelque chose aux Galeries Lafayette*' ('Something's always happening at the Galeries Lafayette'). The accent is on movement, a range of goods that is continually being updated. The brand becomes an event, and the event recalls the brand.

It was then that a new player arrived on the scene, in the form of a modestly sized agency that could be called unusual or even rebellious, run by Anne Storch and

Olivier Aubert ('conceptualist' and 'strategist' respectively, in their own terms), two experienced ad people who have both worked within big businesses but found that this only reinforced their desire for independence. This also explains, at least in part, the striking and singular nature of Aubert Storch Associés Partenaires within the dark forest of ad agencies: by employing only 'creators' (people from the field of theatre of cinema, photographers, graphic designers, all defined by their own style or imaginative world) as opposed to the prosaic 'creatives' generally found in ad agencies, hired to capture the spirit of the time and its images, whose task it is to interpret and work from ideas that already exist.

Philippe Houzé worked with Olivier Aubert on the rebranding of the French supermarket chain Monoprix; Olivier Aubert had collaborated with Jean-Paul Goude on some of his iconic campaigns (such as Orangina); Jean-Paul Goude had, unbeknownst to him, 'blown away' Philippe Houzé with his heroic deeds – from his TV ads to the Bicentennial Parade. Thus the roles were cast, a unique alliance was formed, and from it sprang hundreds of images that studded the decade that followed.

As the literal embodiment of the concept of energy and witty creativity that the store wanted to evoke, what could be a more suitable and universal symbol for a great French store with an international clientele than the mythical and mischievous figure of the chic Parisienne, charming, sexy and feisty? The most famous Frenchwoman of the day, the face of the iconic Marianne, was Laetitia Casta: the ideal locus, one might say, for a concept of Parisian chic that is not that of the avenue Montaigne, nor of department stores, nor of exclusive concept boutiques like Colette, but which retains a little of all of those, yet at the same time remains almost timeless. She provided an image that seemed ready-made for the start of the campaign, one that added media value and whose role grew in strategic importance when the clients agreed, paradoxically, that the campaign would not show their products literally, but instead only metaphorically. This metaphor became a continuing thread as time passed.

CREATION STORIES

this metaphor also had the good fortune of coinciding with one of Jean-Paul Goude's imaginary archetypes; a significant detail for this paradoxical artist who, when he works in advertising, strives to serve the brand or commission but only does so when he can truly make his presence felt. His work is a rare example (although one shared by all the great creators in this field) of the coming together of art and advertising, the 'cultural' and the 'popular'.

It is easy to see similarities between some of the female 'models' in his illustrations, such as the image he creates for Vanessa Paradis in his ads for Chanel, the bird-woman, delicate and mischievous, the chirruping avatar of the Parisian urchin, and the laughing, lively, teasing femininity embodied by Laetitia Casta and the models that followed her in the ads for the Galeries Lafayette.

Dynamism, freshness, wit: these qualities must be placed in context if we are to grasp something of the concept (and the symbolic meaning) that Goude was seeking, and which coincided perfectly with the aims of the store. The dominant contemporary image, driven by some couture designers, was a provocative vision of femininity that was quasi-bestial, violently and graphically sexual, whose heroines will go down in fashion history under the label of 'porno chic'.

Nothing could be a greater contrast, therefore, with the image of Parisian womanhood from *Gigi* and the Moulin Rouge, mingled with the *petits rats* of the Opéra (just across from the Galeries) and the flirtatious *lorettes* of the rue Saint-Georges (a few streets away). A figure that comes from both myth and reality, history and fantasy, from the crossroads of literature and music hall, French novels and Hollywood musicals, and therefore chimes perfectly with the personal mythology of a creator with a dual heritage: Gallic enough to understand and explore the national fascination with this image, yet sufficiently 'foreign' to keep a certain distance and play with the stereotype, handling it with all the irony and freedom required.

Another key component of Goude's world comes into play here: his obsession with dynamics and movement, with rhythm and speed, which springs from (or found its first expression in) his training as a dancer, and his deep grounding in the worlds of film and music. This penchant was just what Philippe Houzé and Olivier Aubert were hoping to find in the new image of the Galeries. The already eloquent 'Something's always happening at the Galeries Lafayette' became, thanks to the shop's general manager Paul Delaoutre, *'Aux Galeries Lafayette, la mode vit plus fort'* ('At the Galeries Lafayette, fashion comes alive'), bringing in images of running and jumping, of bodies that were light, supple and lively, following the rhythm of fashion, which had now become a determining social and cultural force. The images based on this theme took the form of 'moving posters', TV ads just a few seconds long, with editing and soundtrack designed to evoke a race or competition.

Within Goude, two contrary impulses come together simultaneously: this quest for dynamism, and a painstaking interest in composition, detail and finish, the almost classical balance of an image. This 'formalist' streak explains why he also felt the need to 'mess up' his images, stripping them of their frozen and artificial quality by covering them with scrawls and scribbles. This is the source of the unusual lettering, a vital part of the image: it is the work of the graphic designer Yan Stive, who recalled his youthful fascination with graffiti and tagging, and created this cacophonous calligraphy the day before the project presentation by improvising with a computer mouse, in order to scratch and shake up the image. The left-handed ductus of the designer adds just the right touch of angularity and (artificial) awkwardness. There is no place in this ensemble for an intrusive logo: it is the entire image that becomes the emblem of the store, recognizable at a glance.

*

As mentioned above, the directors of Galeries Lafayette accepted the disappearance of the product in favour of the brand: the (apparent) removal of the logo in favour of the image as a whole was also approved, which in fact paradoxically serves to make the logo more visible by its absence. There was a further challenge left, perhaps even riskier within the world of advertising, a world of impermanence and obligatory and enforced innovation: to allow the campaign to develop over time, to see it as a long process of change (one that perfectly suits Goude's temperament, used as he is to coming back to the same motif again and again, changing it, moving it, transforming it, like a patient and creative craftsman). This approach stands in contradiction to the theory of endless eye-catching advocated by advertising dogma.

The hundreds of images that have resulted over the last decade are proof of how successfully this challenge was embraced. They have become another gripping storyline among the many that Goude has created around himself, and around his muses (Toukie, Grace Jones, Farida). They have taken their place in a long and proud tradition of French advertising posters (Olivier Aubert believes that only France, Great Britain and Japan escape from the rigid formatting and flat codification of American advertising imagery). They are the heirs of the swirling illustrations that Mucha created for Job, and posters created by Cappiello for Fumigène, Cassandre for L'Étoile du Nord, Savignac for Monsavon, Villemot for Orangina, and Gruau (of whom Goude is particularly fond) for Dior. (Great Britain, on the other hand, produced many great poster artists, such as Eric Ravilious and Edward Bawden, but they generally vanish behind their work: memorable posters for Lyons Tea or the railways stations of Metroland may remain, but their creators remain relatively unknown.)

In today's increasingly muddy landscape of high culture and low culture, craft and design, contemporary art and media buzz, these images occupy a place apart. Appearing in a variety of sizes (from brochures to billboards), coming and going as the seasons change, pasted on the walls of Métro stations or shining out from the pages of a magazine, they are engraved on our memories, as vivid and untouchable as an afterimage on the eye, forming a witty and ironic chronicle of passing time for a whole generation.

The Hat, work in progress. Philip Treacy's studio, London, 2000.

P

erhaps more so than for any other product, the brand image of a store plays a vital role: it determines, shifts, focuses and adjusts the store's identity and through it, its customer base and their sociological make-up.

It was therefore a stimulating challenge for Jean-Paul Goude, particularly given his prior achievements in the realm of advertising, from posters to pop videos, to accept the offer (made by Philippe Houzé) of rebranding the store, and therefore becoming part of its richly creative history.

Certainly no one could have predicted that an association of this kind, particularly within the ephemeral world of advertising, would last for so long.

This book looks back on this ten-year adventure, telling the tale behind the image, step by step. It is much more than a simple retrospective, cataloguing and commemorating the campaigns that over time have paraded across walls and magazine pages. Instead, it is about showing a method, a personal approach, all the stages of working from the first scribbled notes on a scrap of paper to the finished product, as well as the indecision, regrets, chance discoveries, amendments and adjustments along the way.

It is what Goude sees as a long line of stories, giving readers a glimpse into the strange mechanisms at work behind any act of creation, even though the public normally only sees the results in their most polished and perfected form, for it is only this that will succeed in capturing the gaze of passers-by (or readers) in a hurry, and only this that will linger in their memories as a faint but lasting trace.

Following pages: Laetitia Casta, 2001.

SO CHIC

Window projects, sketches, 2001.

Opposite: Laetitia Casta,
poster *in situ*, 2001.

23

Mode de mars, preliminary sketch, 2001.

Window project, preliminary sketch, 2001.

Mode de mars, preliminary sketch and final version. 2001.

Following pages: *Semaine du blanc* (bedlinen promotion),
preliminary sketch and final version. 2002.

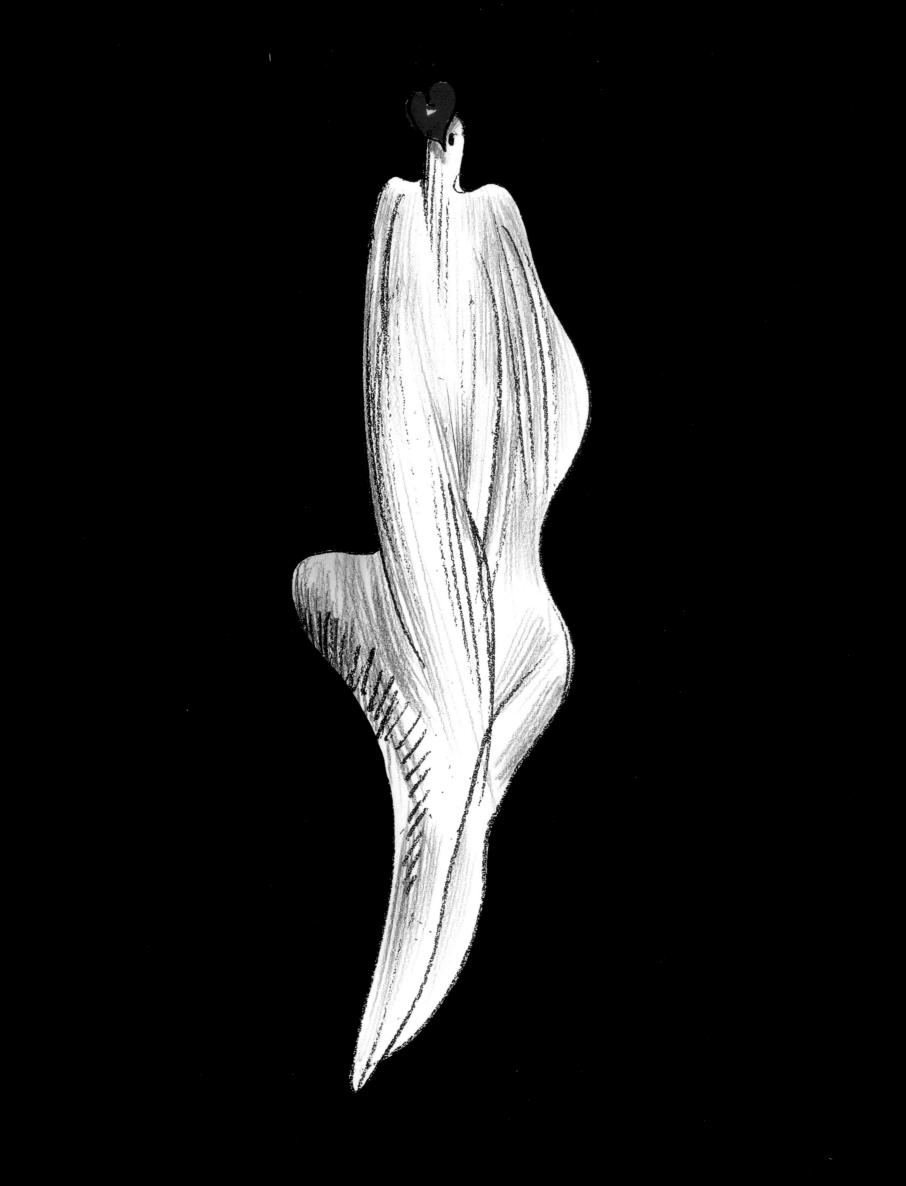

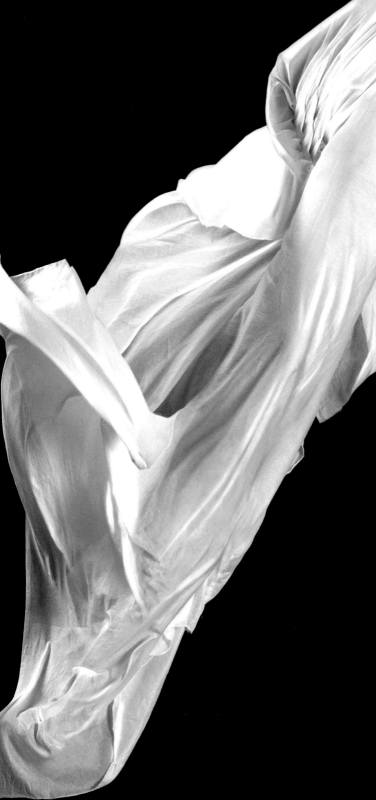

Opposite: *Les Galeries Lafayette s'agrandissent*
(Galeries Lafayette are expanding), 2003.
Below: project for *Lafayette Palace*, 2004.

EVERYTHING'S GOT TO GO

Les Soldes (The Sales), preliminary sketches, 2001 and 2005.

Soldes (Sales), original image, 2001.

Soldes (Sales), revised version, 2003.

Semaine fantastique,
promotional campaign, inspiration
and final image, 2001.
Following pages:
Soldes (Sales), final image, 2005.

37

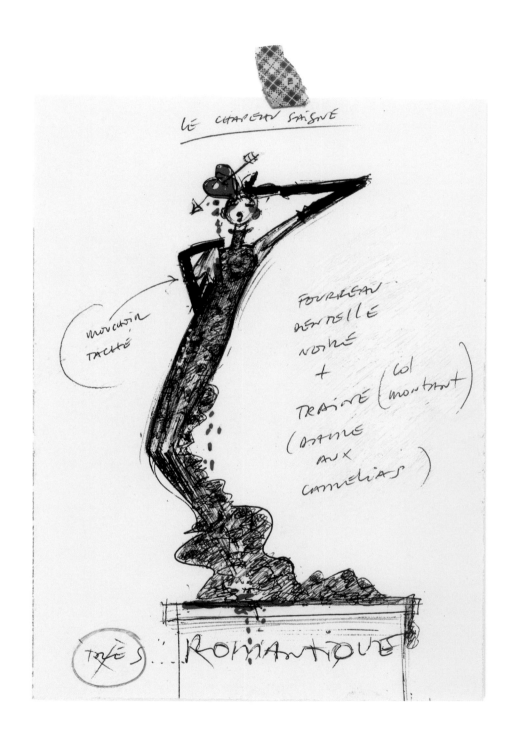

Mode romantique, preliminary sketch and final image, 2001.

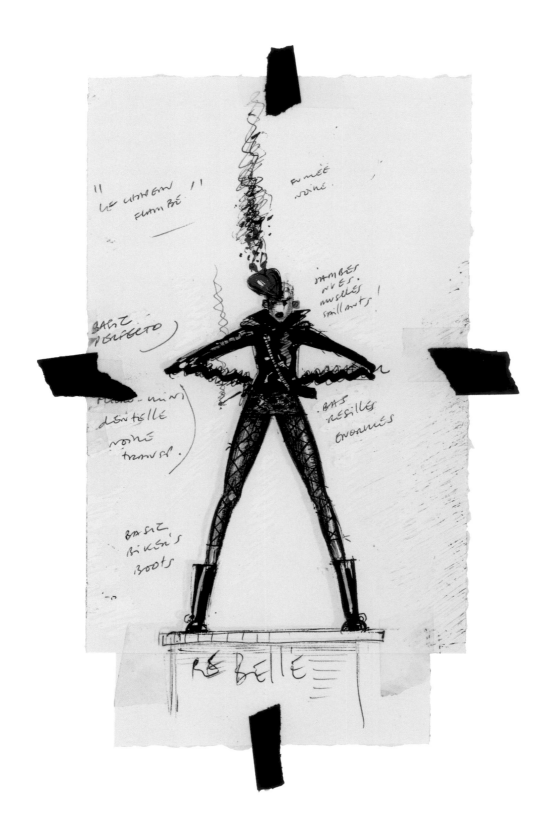

Mode rebelle, preliminary sketch and final image. 2001.

Opposite: *Soldes*, 2004.

Prix cœur, promotional
campaign, 2005.

tulle

tulle plisse

Les 3J, promotional campaign.
Above: *The Supremes*, inspiration; opposite: final image, 2001.

Opposite, *Move expo*, promotional campaign, 2001.

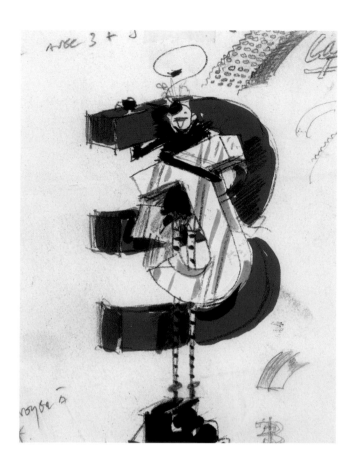

Les 3J, preliminary sketch and final image, 2005.
Following pages: *Les 3J* in situ.

AMAZONS AND BARBARIANS

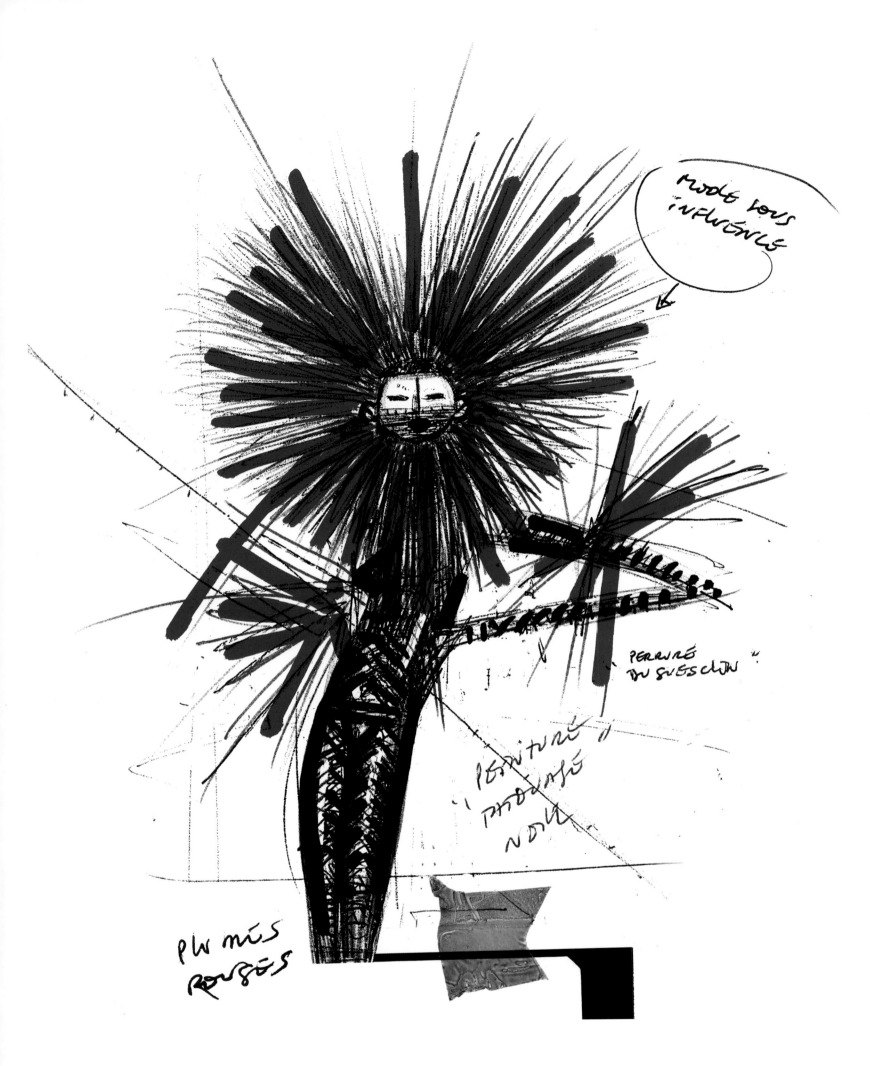

L'Amazone, promotional campaign, preliminary sketch, 2002.

L'Amazone, sketch, 2002.

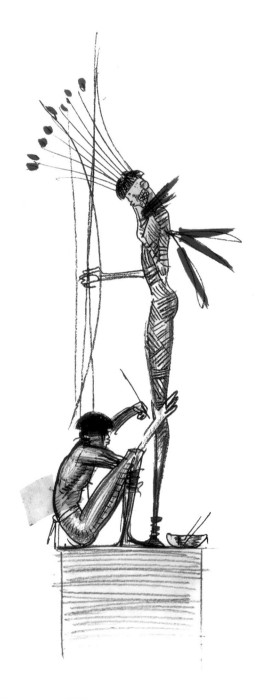

Opposite: *L'Amazone*, poster *in situ*, 2002.

"J'AI TOUJOURS ENVIE
D'ALLER AUX GALERIES"

GALERIES
Lafayette

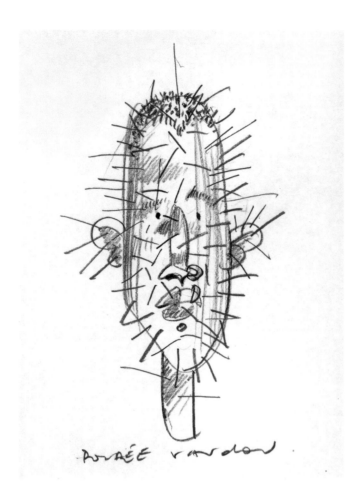

Mode barbare, above: *poupée vaudou* (voodoo doll), sketch; below and opposite: preliminary sketches, 2002.

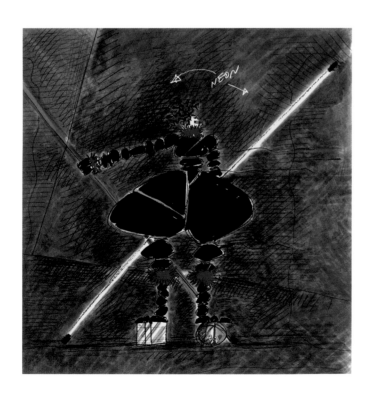

Following pages: *Mode barbare*, preliminary sketch and final image, 2002.

HEATWAVE

Mode d'été (Blanca Li),
promotional campaign, 2006.
Following pages: *Bains de mer*,
preliminary sketches, 2001

Bain de mer
couture.

Bass in
de
Glace

SUMMER'S TALES

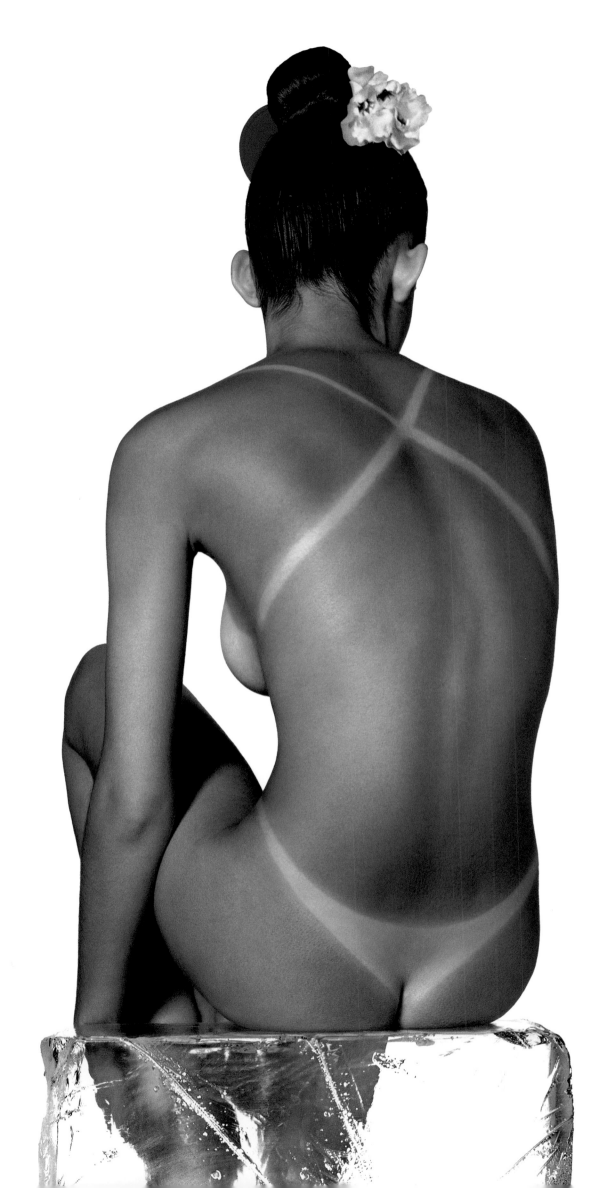

Preceding page: *Bains de mer*, final image, 2001.

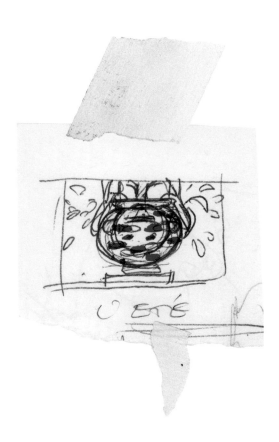

Mode d'été, sketch, 2001.

Opposite, *Mode d'été*, poster *in situ*, 2001.

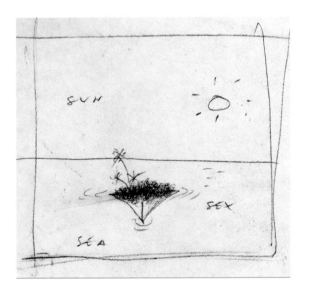

Bains de mer, promotional campaign,
sketches and poster *in situ,* 2005.

Bains de mer, preliminary sketch and poster *in situ*, 2002.

Following pages: *Mode d'été*, poster, 2003.
Bains de mer, preliminary sketch, 2003.

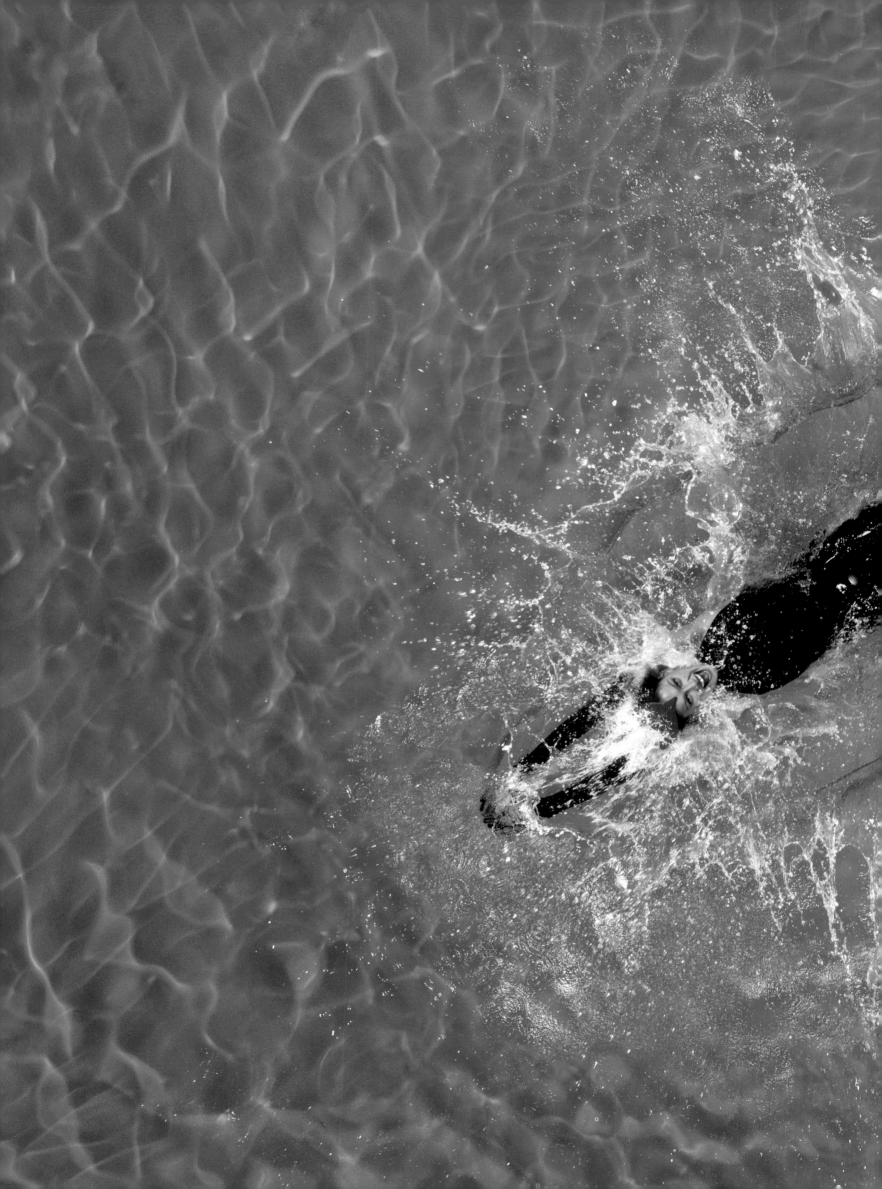

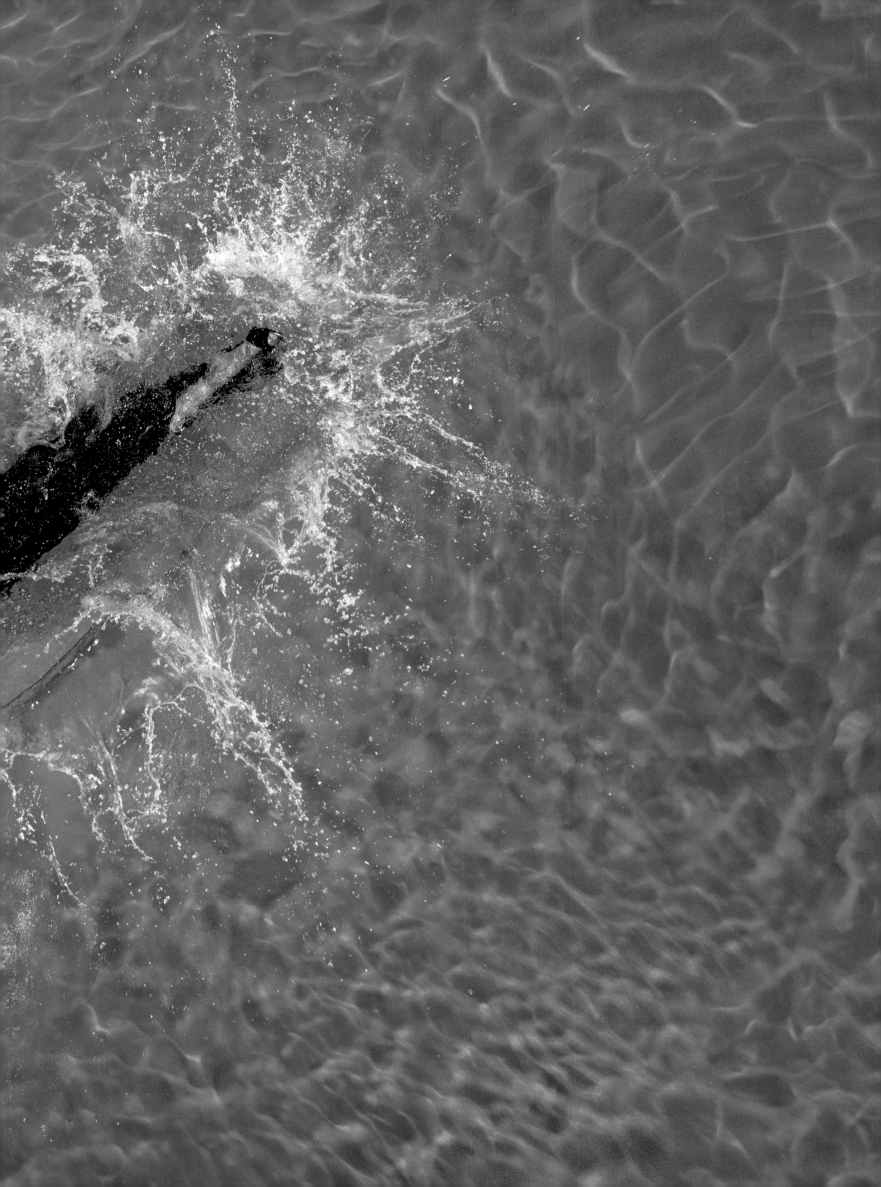

MY FAIR LADY

Le mariage, preliminary sketch, 2001.
Following pages: preliminary sketch 2004 and final image 2001.

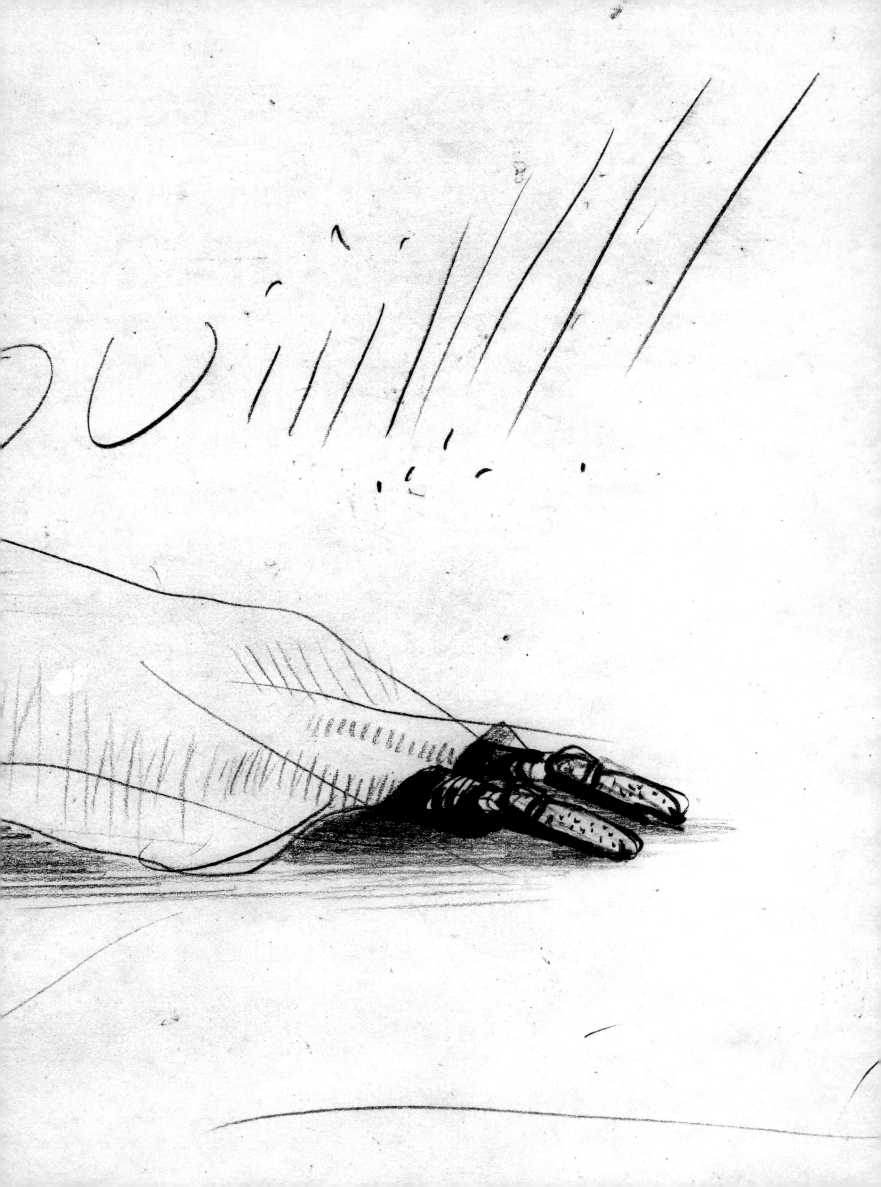

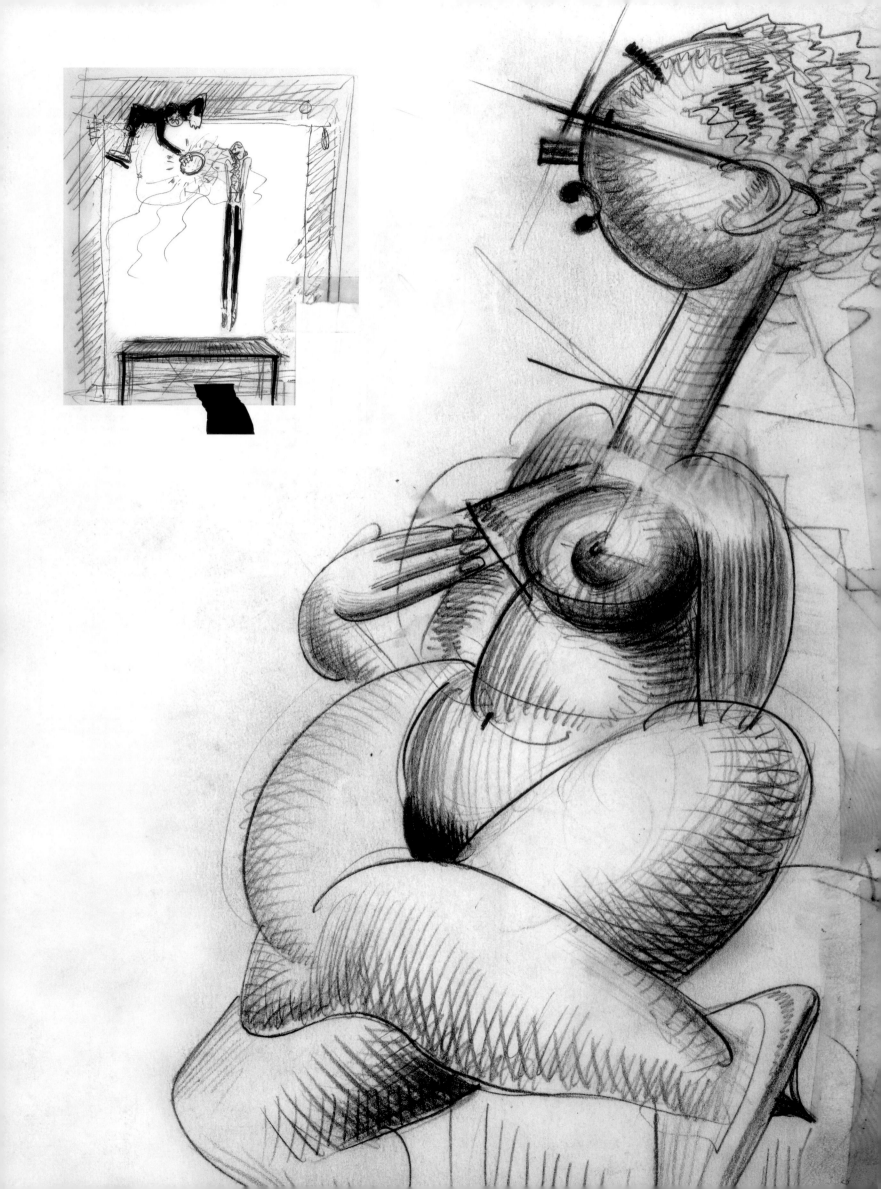

Le mariage, preliminary sketches 2005
and 2003. Opposite: final image 2005.

EAST MEETS WEST

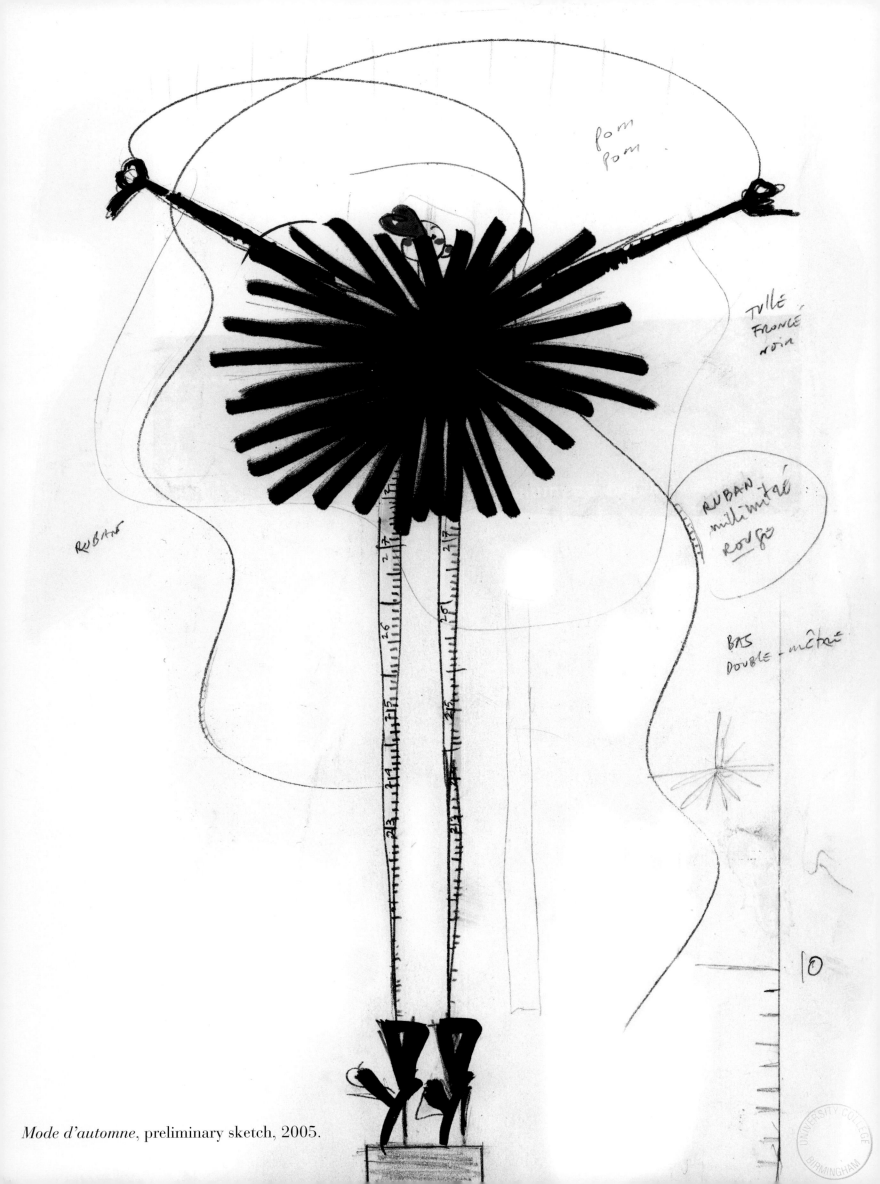

Mode d'automne, preliminary sketch, 2005.

Chine, promotional campaign sketch, 2003.

Opposite: *Mode d'automne*, final image, 2005.

Chine, promotional campaign, preliminary sketches, 2003.

Opposite: *Chine*, final poster, 2003.

PHOTO
LAETITIA

Preceding pages:
Mode de Mars, sketches, 2003.

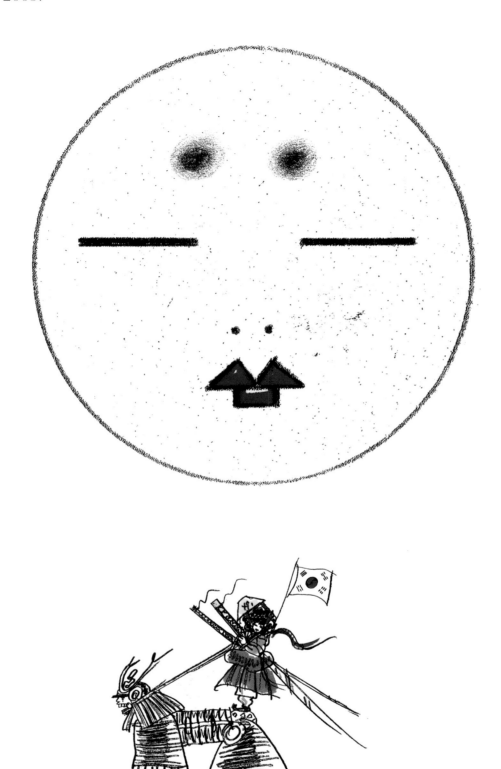

Asiatic, sketches for promotional campaign, 2004.

Opposite: *Ruban* (Ribbon), sketch, 2003.

Generic promotional campaign,
final image and poster *in situ*, 2009.

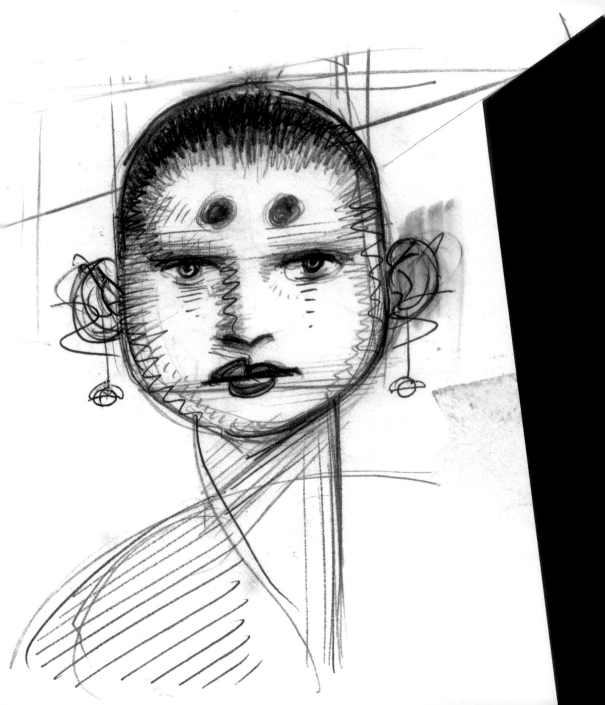

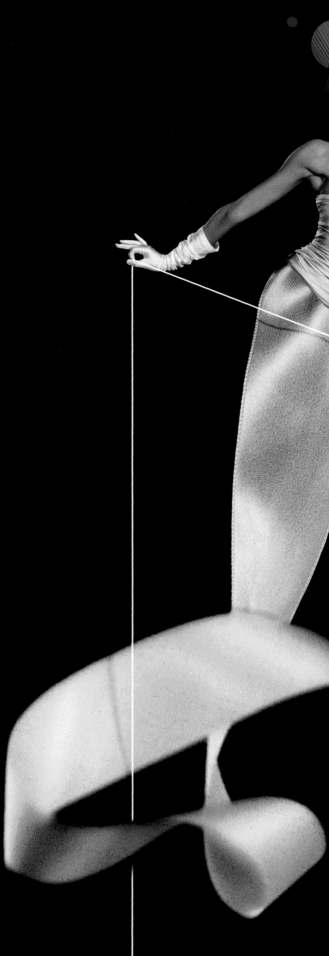

Traveller Chic, sketch and final image, 2008.

106

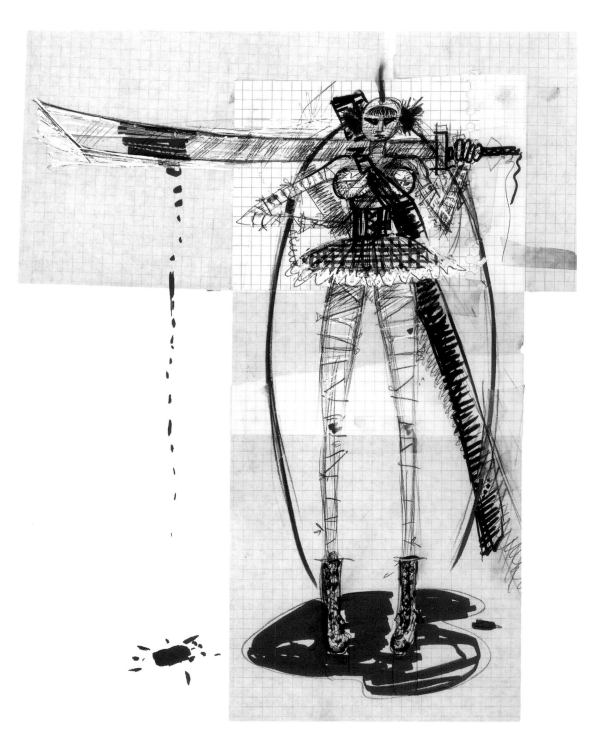

Asiatic, promotional campaign. Top: wounded sword.
Above: sketch. Opposite: final image, 2008.

Following pages: *Asiatic*, poster *in situ*, 2008.

MEN AND WOMEN

Mode porte-bonheur, final image, 2005.
Following pages: *Jeans Tonic*, preliminary sketches, 2002.

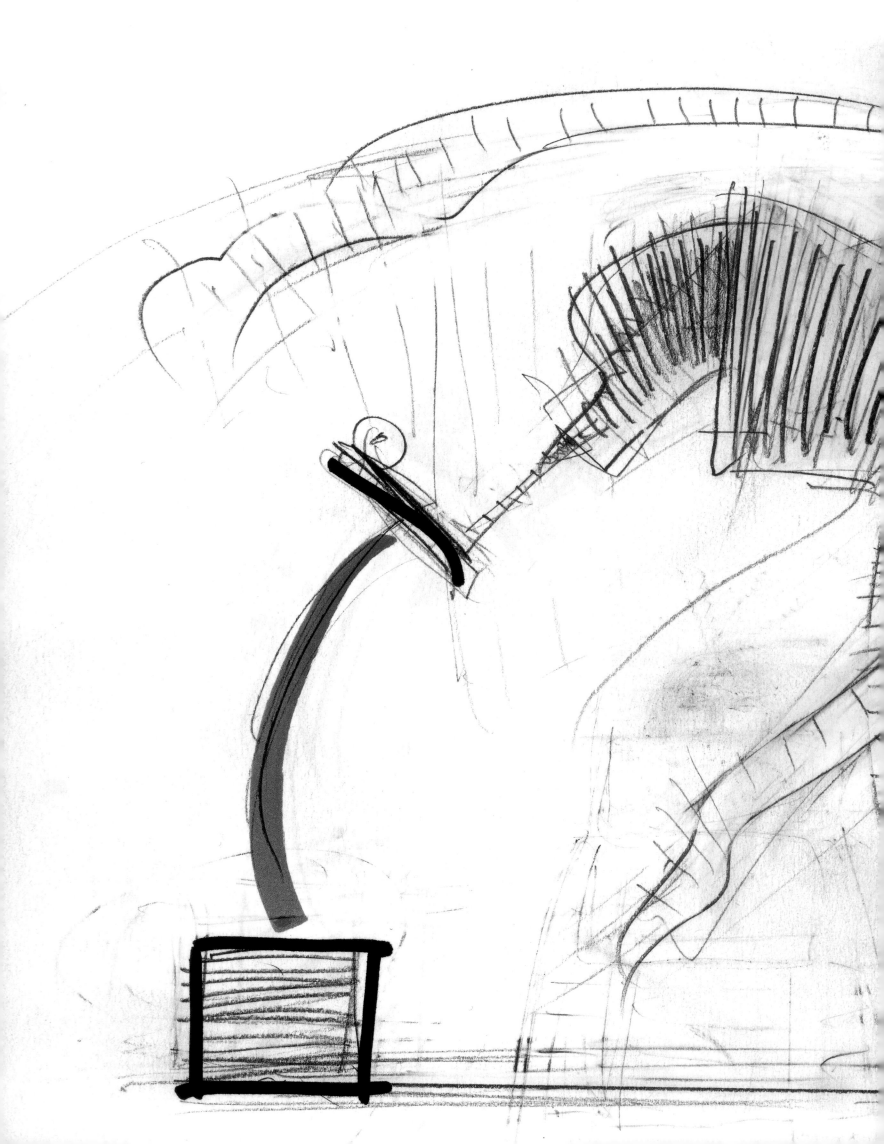

Ballon

BASKET-ball

Opposite: *Bollywood* (Rukmini Chaterjee),
final image, 2005.

Brésil, final image, 2005.

Following pages, *La mode vit plus fort*,
sketches and poster *in situ*, 2005.

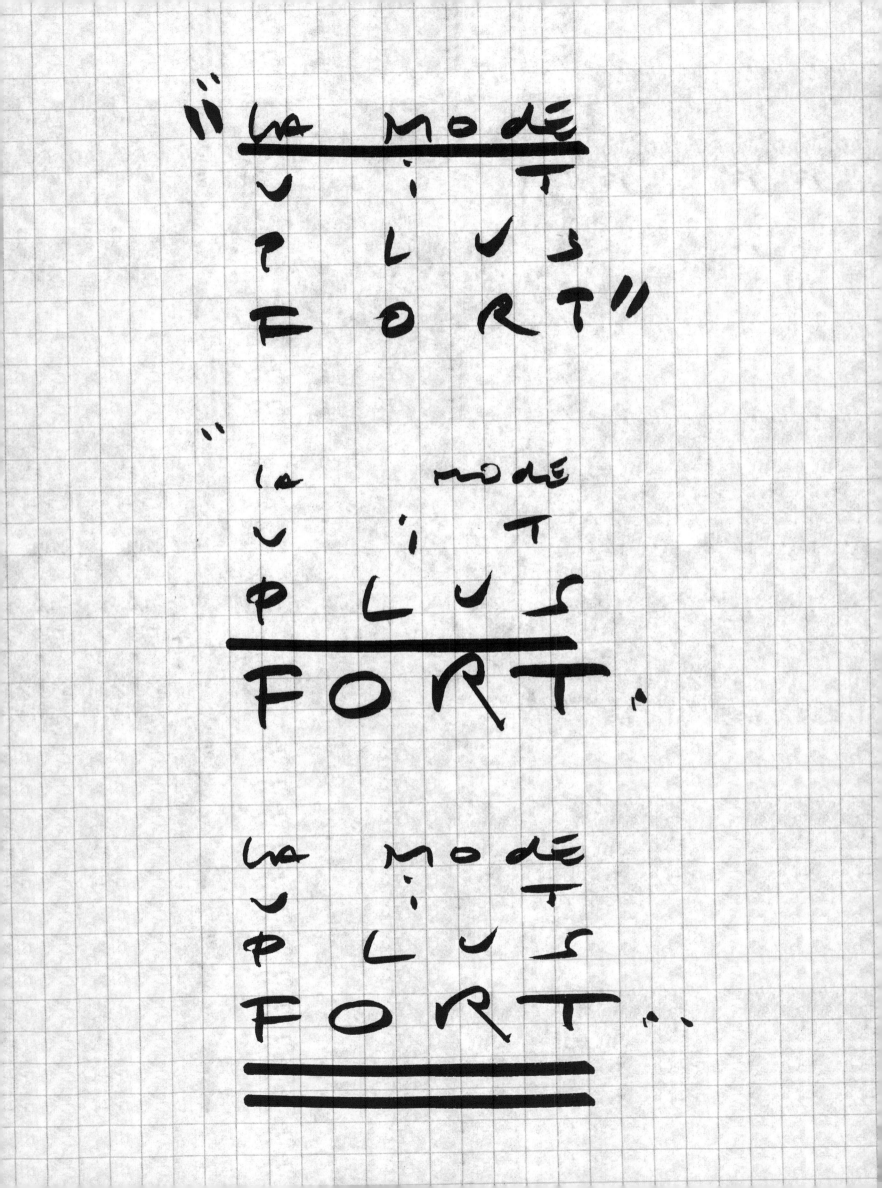

FASHION ANIMALS

Anna Piaggi, inspiration for the campaign
Bêtes de Mode (Fashion Animals).

Métamorph'osez,
preliminary sketches, 2003.

Opposite: *Bêtes de Mode* (Fashion Animals),
final image, 2006.

MEN

Above and following pages:
L'Homme, sketch and variations, 2004.

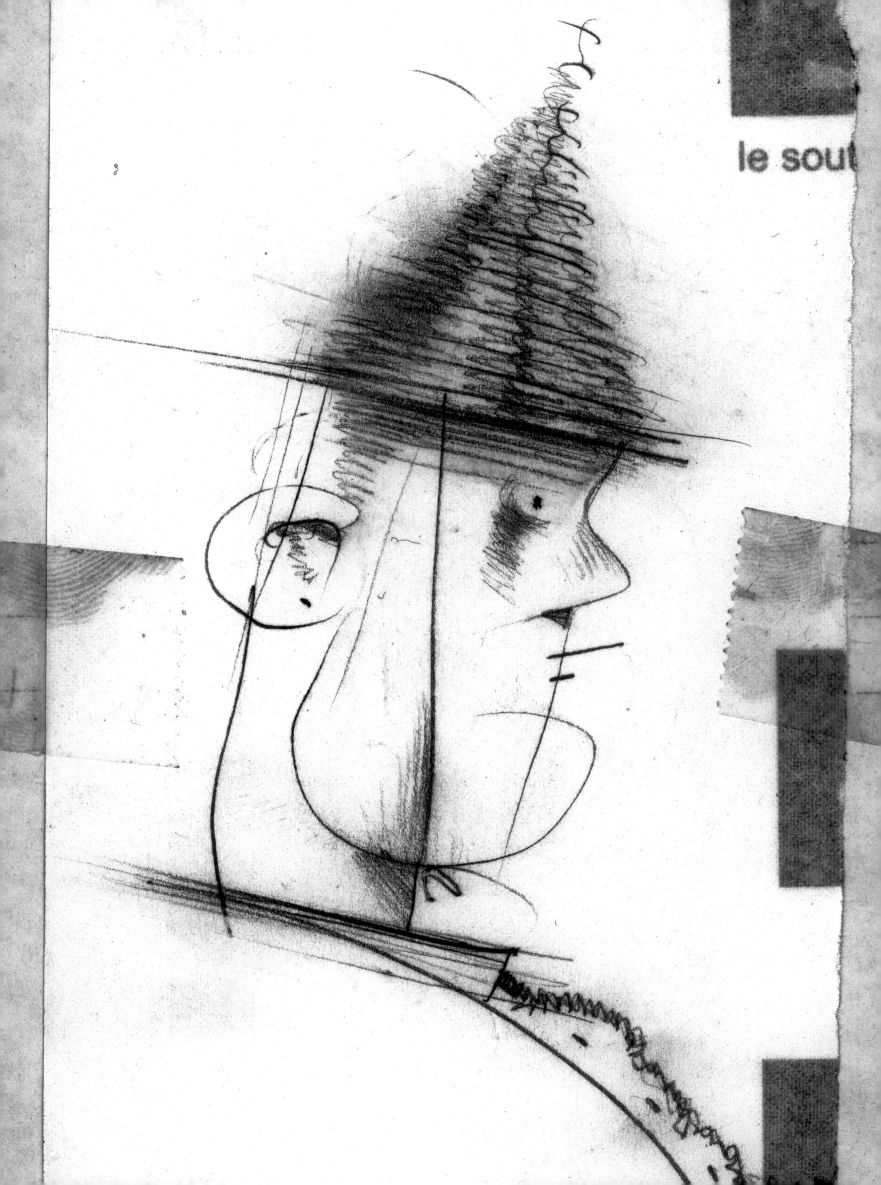

le sout

Above and following pages: *L'Homme* (Laetitia Casta revised),
preliminary sketch, collage and final image, 2003.

Opposite: *L'Homme*, poster *in situ*, 2007.

99f, film after the novel by
Frédéric Beigbeder.

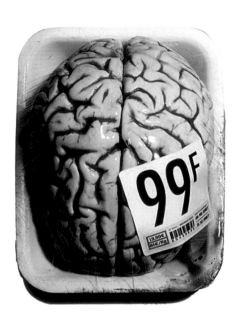

99f, publicity material.

L'Homme, preliminary sketch and self-portrait, 2003.

L'Homme (Jun Miyake),
poster and preliminary sketch, 2009.

HOME SWEET HOME

La Maison, preliminary sketch, 2008.

Following pages: *La Maison*, preliminary sketch and final image, 2004.

La Maison, poster, first version and sketches, 2008.

La Maison, poster, final version *in situ*, 2008
and preliminary sketches, 2004 and 2001.

La Maison, spring, preliminary sketch and final image, 2006.

La Maison, autumn,
preliminary sketch and final image, 2006.

Following pages: *La Maison*, winter, preliminary sketch, 2004.

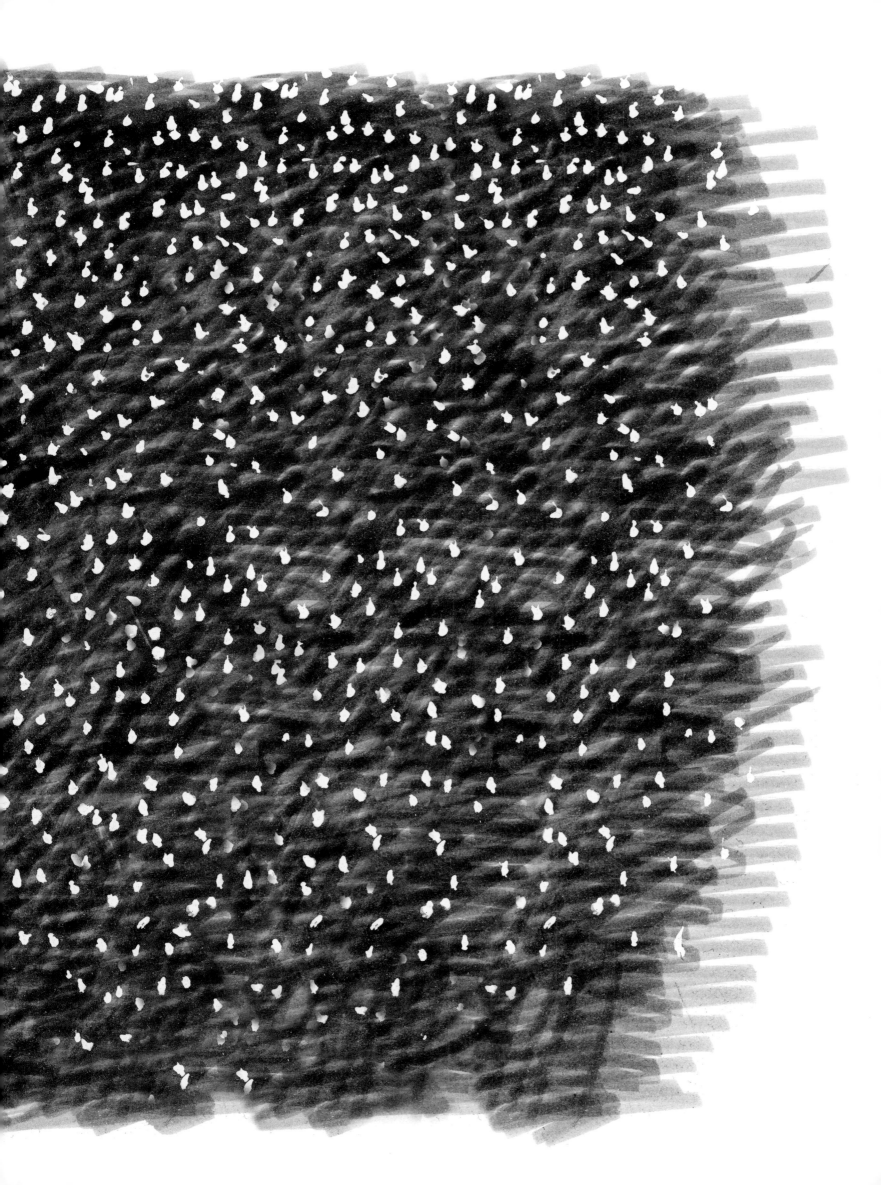

La Maison, preliminary sketch and final image, 2002.

THIS SPORTING LIFE

La Mode et le sport, final image, 2004.
Following pages: poster *in situ*, 2004.

"J'AI TOUJOURS ENVIE
D'ALLER AUX GALERIES"
GALERIES
Lafayette
SPORT

La Mode et le sport, sketches, 2004.

Opposite: *La Mode vit plus sport*, poster *in situ*, 2005.

Danse avec la mode (Mia Frye),
preliminary sketches and final image, 2008.

LA MODE VIT PLUS SPORT

Retro Chic, preliminary sketch, 2004.
Following pages:
La mode vit plus fort, publicity film,
storyboard and stills, 2005.

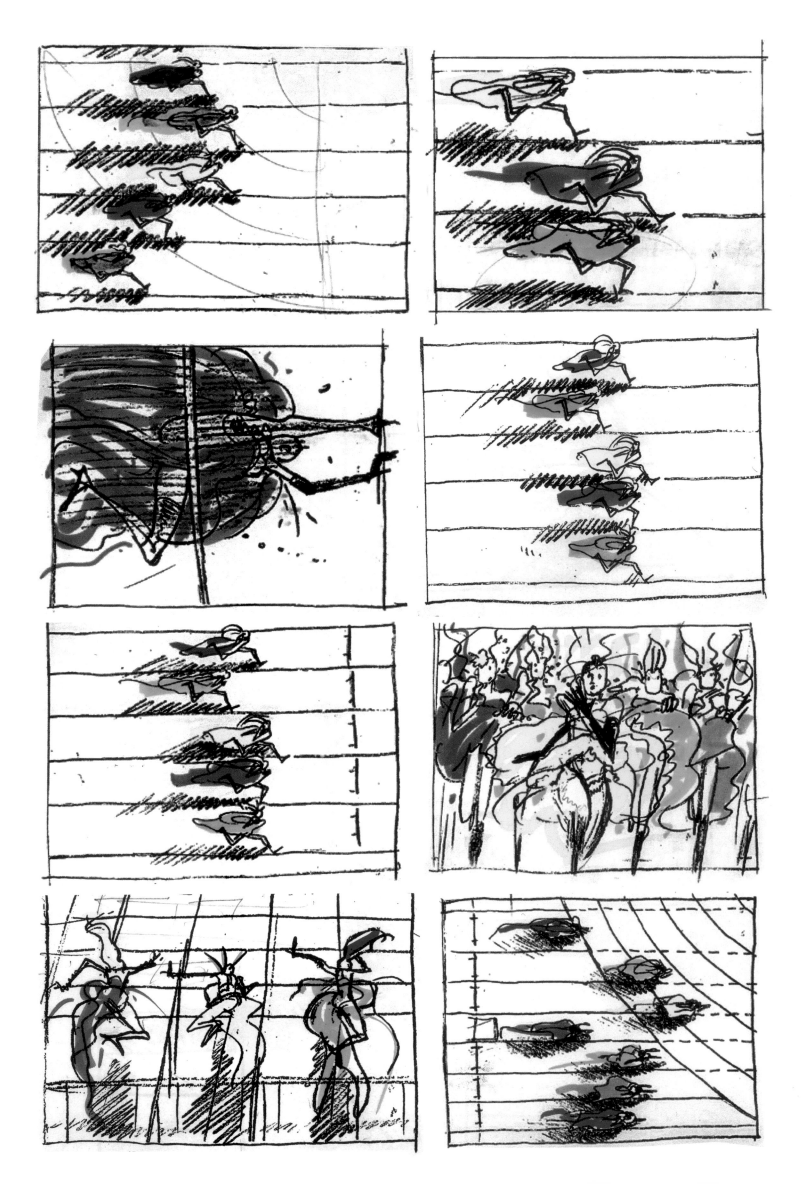

300m (1)

UNDRESSING UP

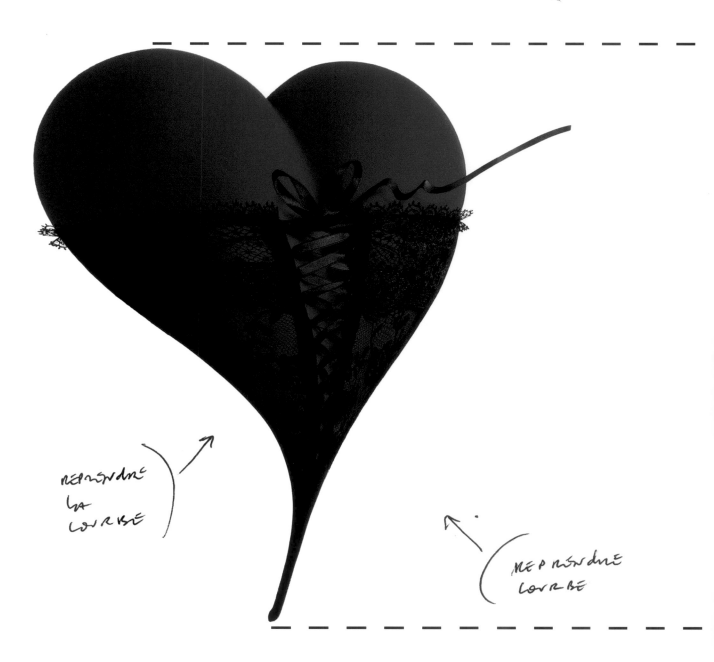

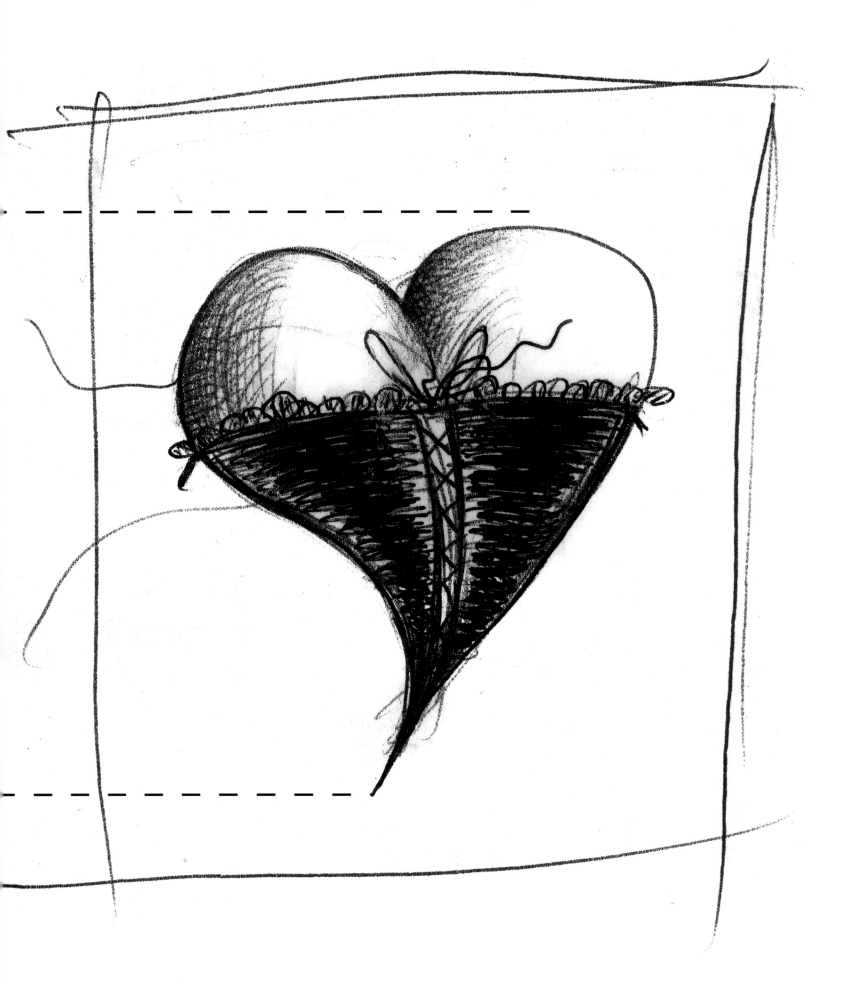

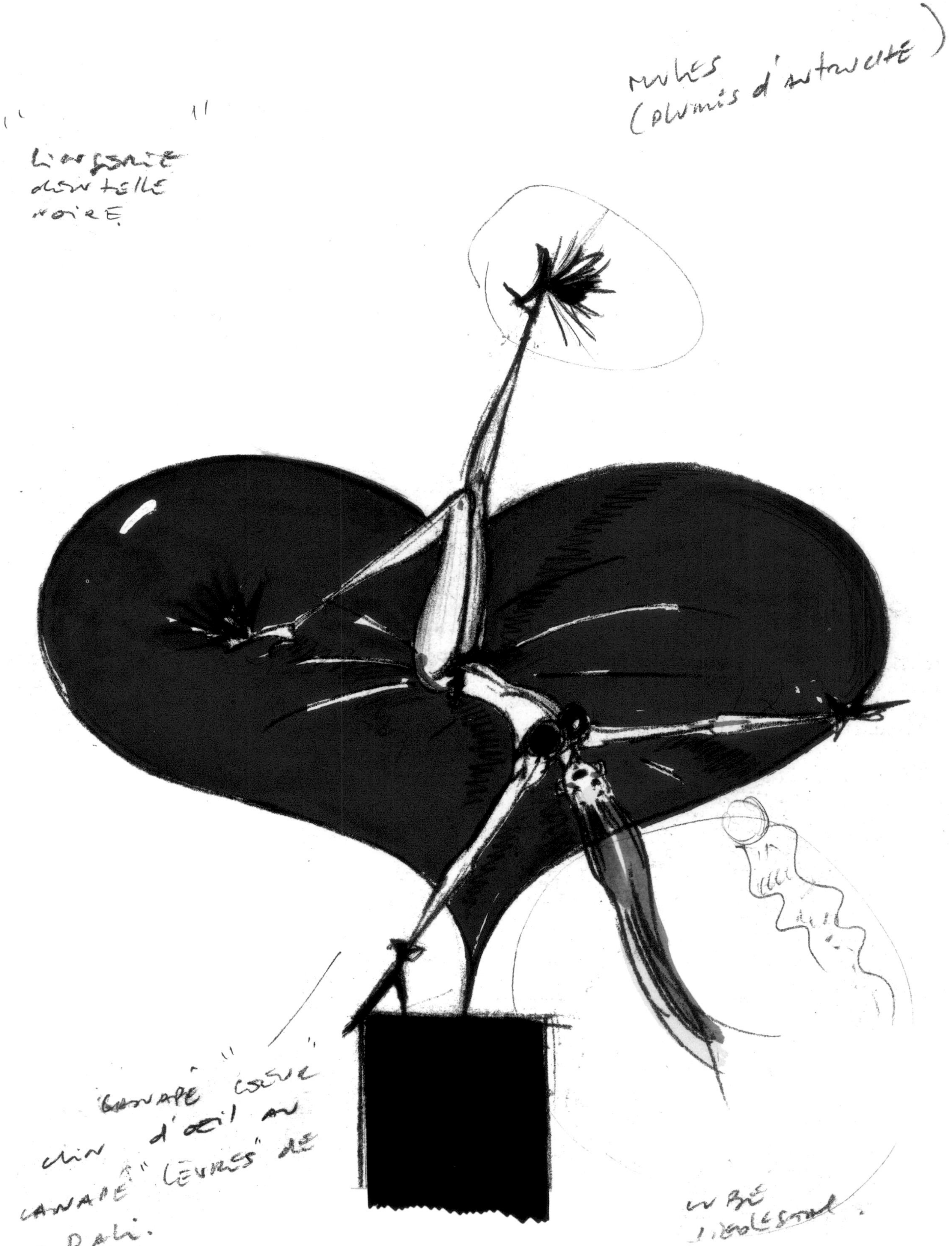
Lingerie dentelle noire
mules (plumes d'autruche)
"Canapé cœur" clin d'œil au canapé "lèvres" de S. Dali.

Preceding pages: *Lingerie*, sketches and final image, 2001.

Lingerie, preliminary sketch and poster *in situ*, 2003.

Opposite, this page and following pages: *Lingerie*, final image and sketches, 2002.

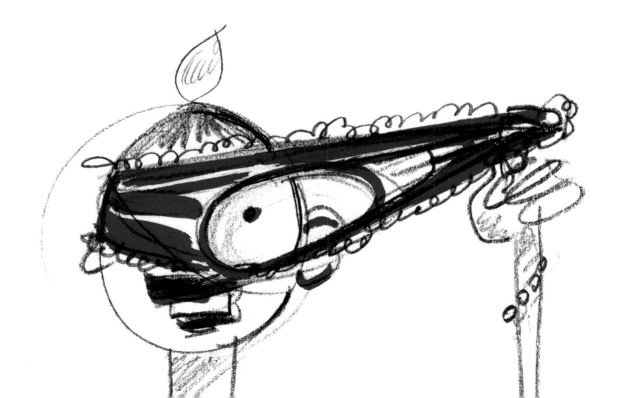

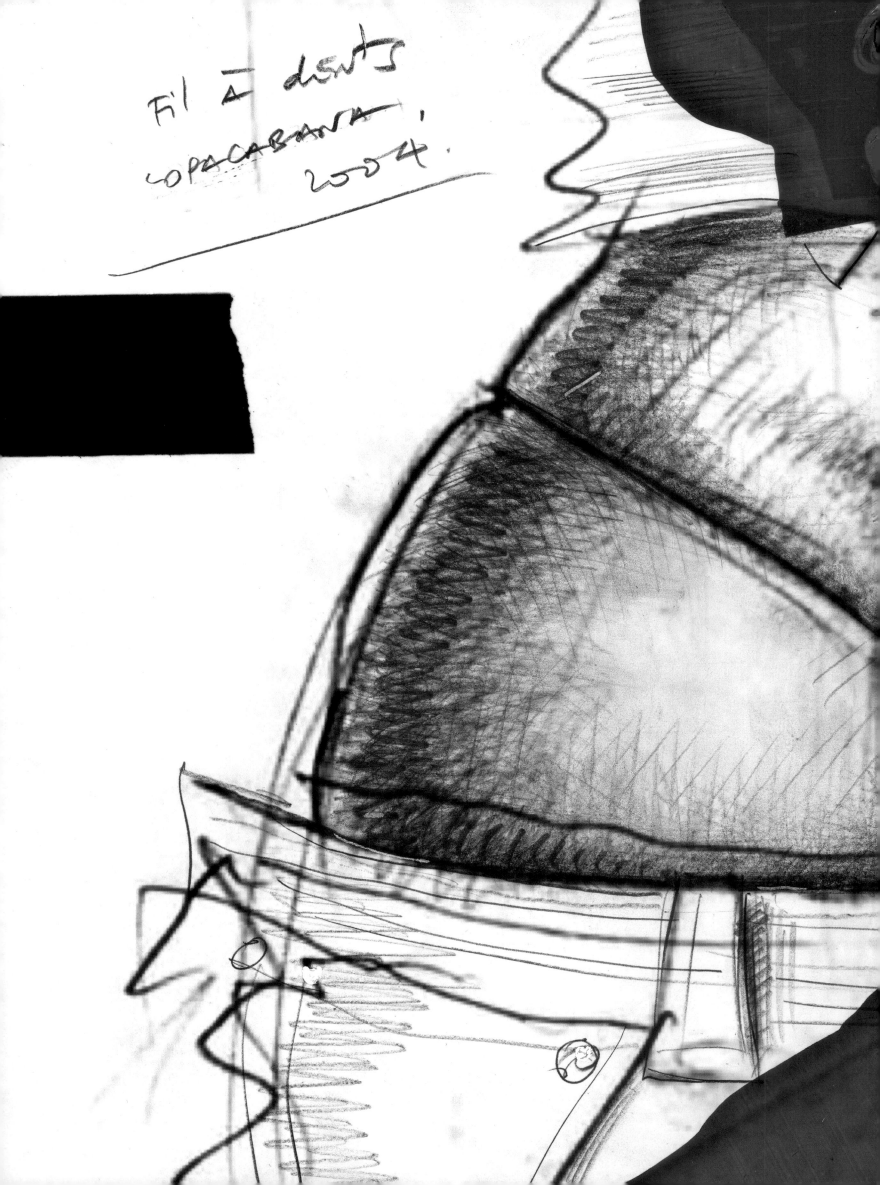

LARGER THAN LIFE

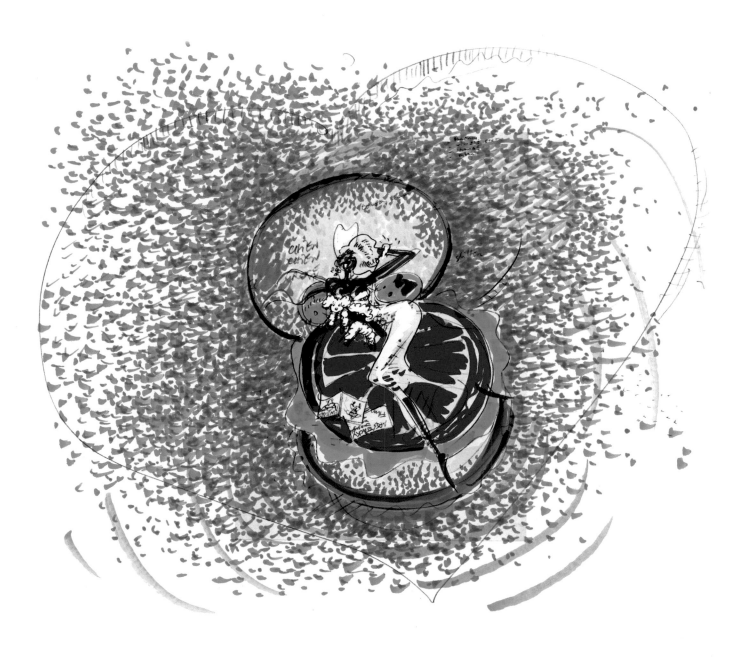

Los Angeles Fashion, preliminary sketch, 2006.

Hamburger bed, Esquire magazine, 1972.

Hamburger bed revised: *Los Angeles Fashion*, final image, 2006.

Ciné-Mode, final image and sketch, 2003.

Lætitia Casta vue par Jean-Paul Goude

Opposite: *Rentrée des classes* (Back to school), poster *in situ*, 2002.
Below: *Fête des mères* (Mother's Day), final image, 2002.

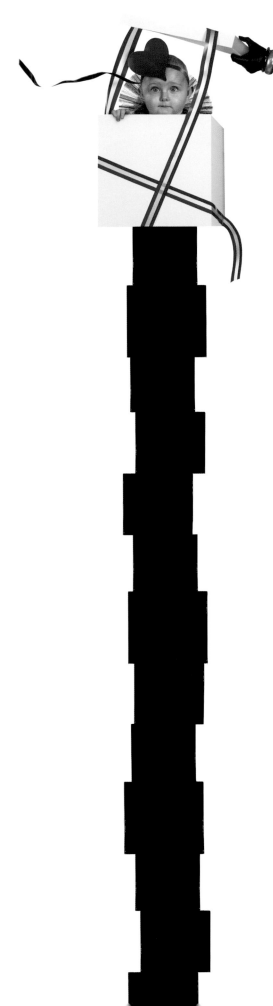

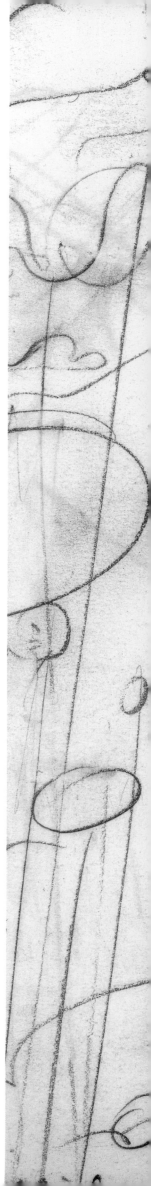

Above: *Jungle d'Eden*, final image, 2007.
Opposite: *L'air de Paris*, preliminary sketch, 2002.

Quoi de neuf? (What's new?), preliminary sketches, 2003, and final image, 2008.

YUM YUM

MIAM  MIAM

MIAM

Preceding page, opposite and above:
Gourmet, sketch and variations, 2003.

201

Gourmet, preliminary sketch and poster, 2005.

WINTER'S TALES

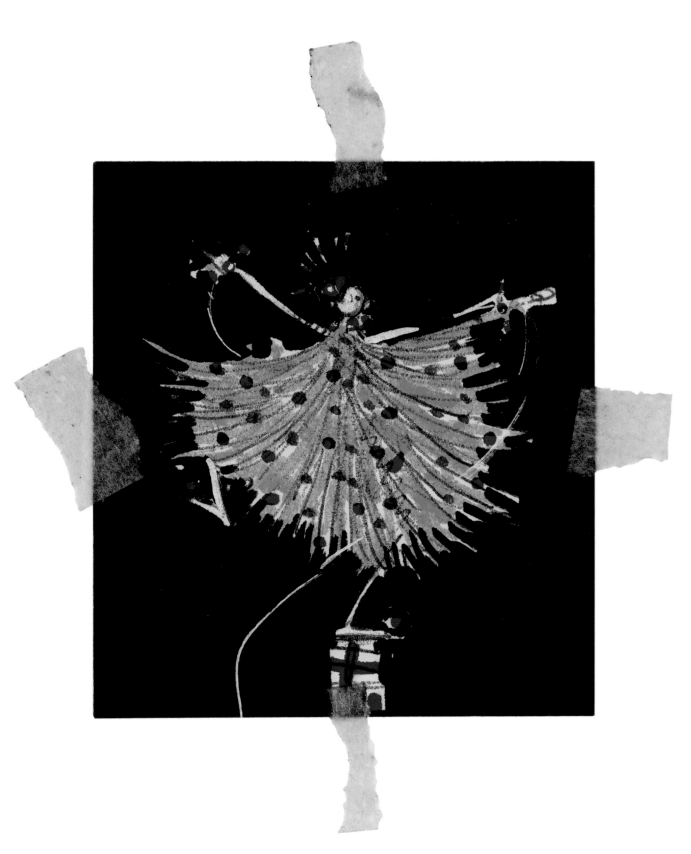

Noël, sketch, 2001.

Noël, preliminary sketch, 2001 and *Noël Royal*, final image, 2005.

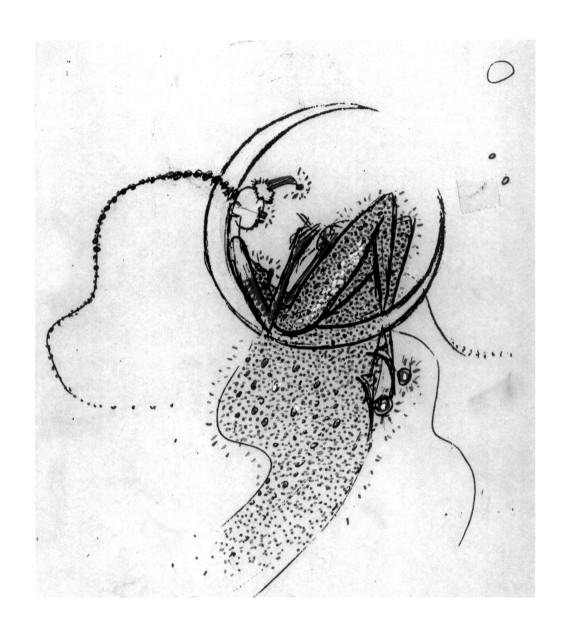

Cher papa Noël (Dear Santa), preliminary sketch and final image, 2002.

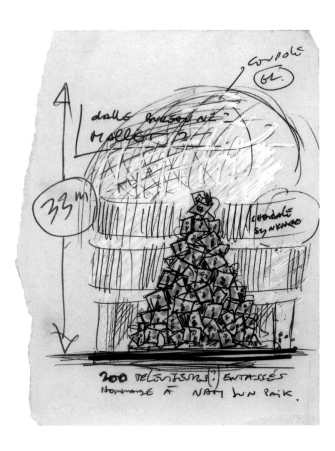

Noël de rêve (Dream Christmas).
Top: sketch; above: proposed store
installation; opposite: preliminary sketch;
following page: final image, 2006.

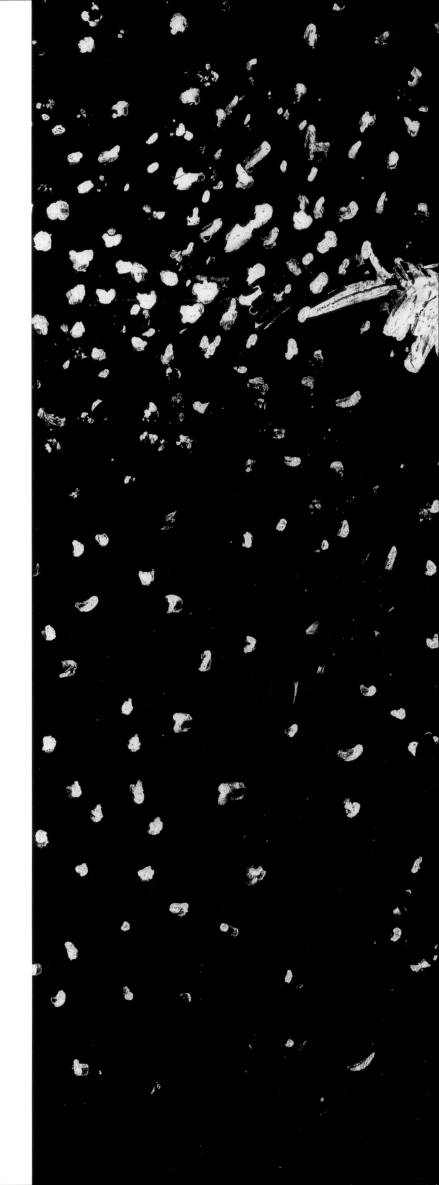

PARIS VIT PLUS FORT

Generic image, sketch, 2001.

Above: generic image.
Opposite: poster *in situ*.
Below: *Le jouet* (Toy promotion),
final image. 2005.

Following pages: sketch variation. 2005.

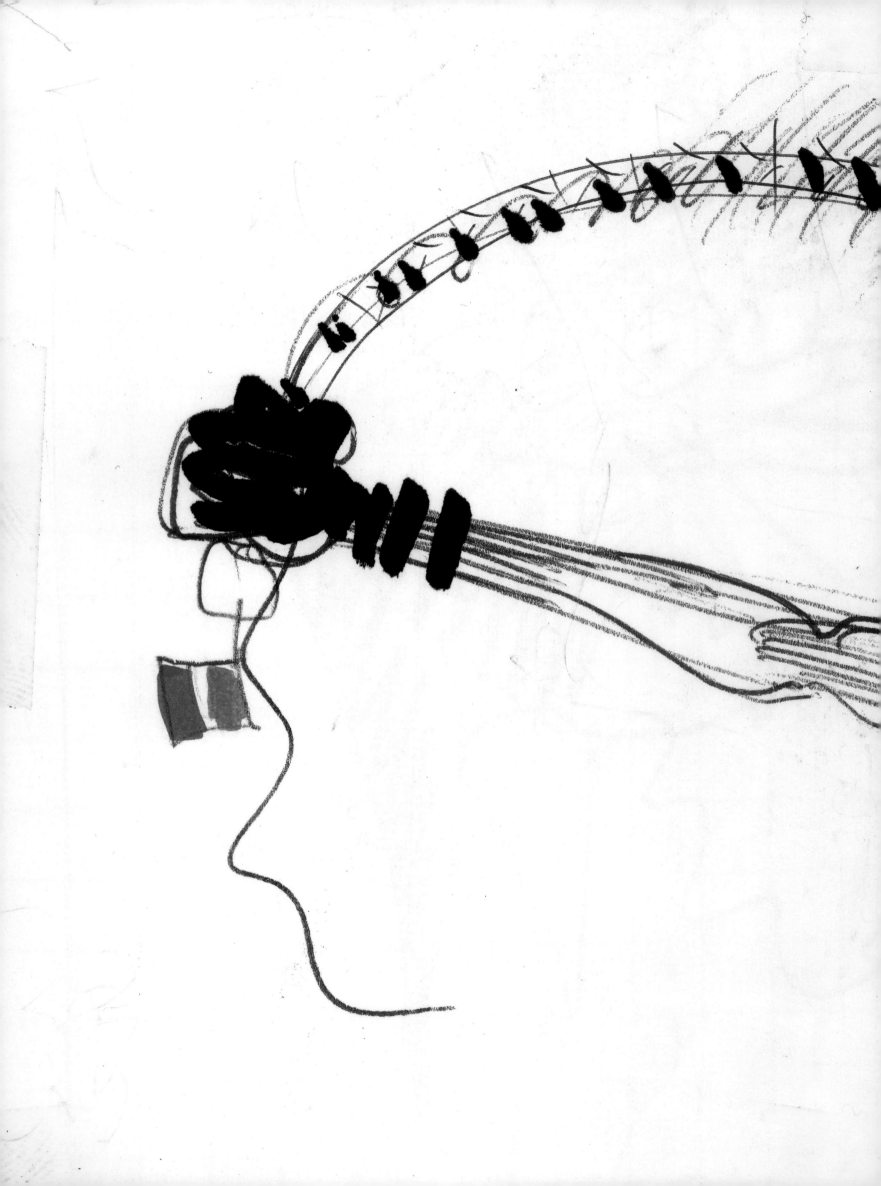

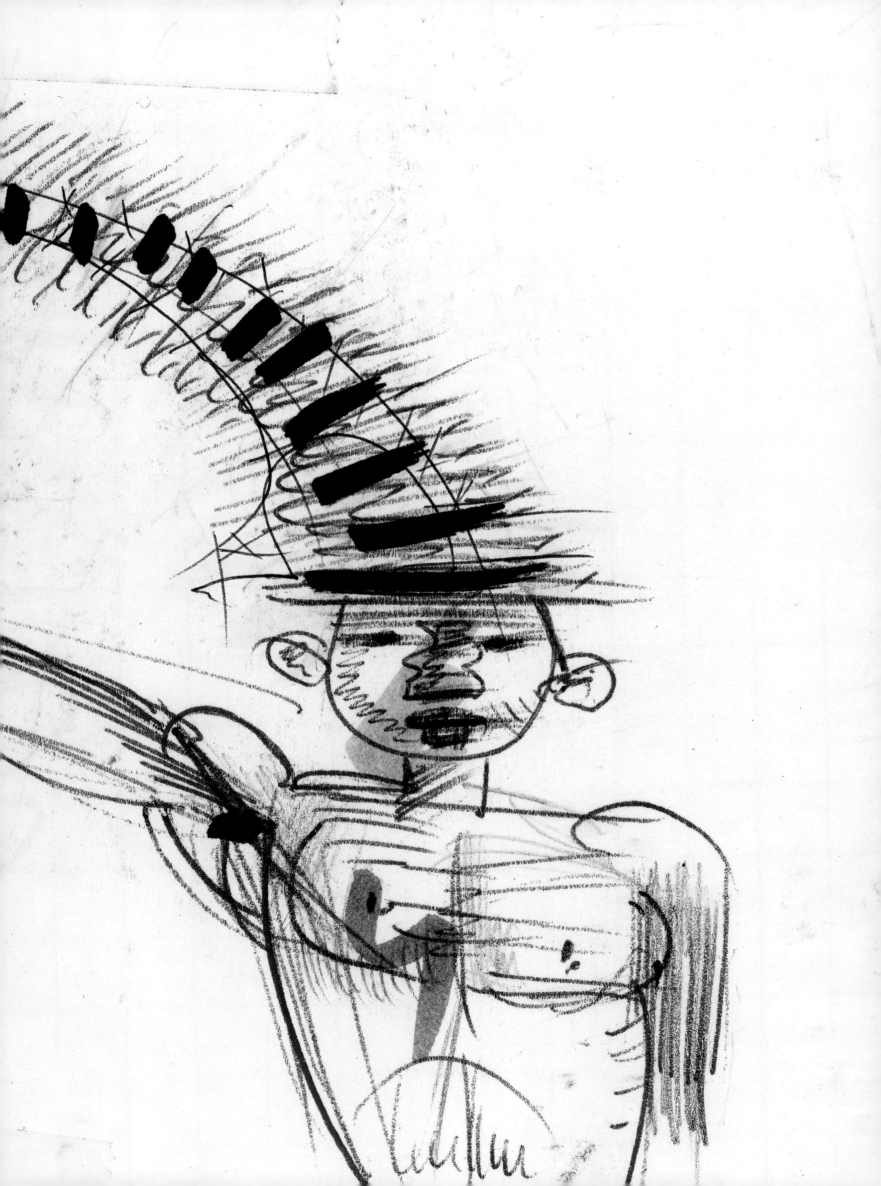

220

LA FRANCE

Thanks

Special thanks to Marion Pinell and Yan Stive
for their collaboration.

Additional thanks to:

Philippe Houzé, Paul Delaoutre, Michel Rouleau, Gérard Lafargue, Philippe Lemoine,
Brigitte Bost, Alexandra Rocca Simon, Anne-Marie Schwaab, Béatrice Rollet,
Anne-Marie Verdin, Marie Petracco, Isabelle Mercier, Marie-Noëlle Joly,
Sophie Brossier, Anne-Marie Gaultier.

Olivier Aubert, Anne Storch, Régine Leduc, Florence Duvivier,
Nelly David, Fabienne Bailly.

Philippe Baumann, Franck Joyeux, Virginie Laguens, Frédéric Godefroy,
Mustapha Khelfa, Gérard Stérin, Jean-François Pinto, Marie Beltrami,
Alex Aiku, Blue Marine, Inge Grognard, Isabelle Luzet, Dee Dee Dorzee,
Laurent Philippon, Nathalie Cambessedes, Nicolas Premoli, Do Won Kim,
Vanessa Lena, Alice Nez, Clarisse Barthélemy, Stefan Bartlett, Nina Tryon,
James Kaliardos, Guillaume Riboullet, Isabelle Revert, Hélène Chauvet,
Françoise Aghulon, Yves Boujenah, Michel Hardy, Francine Bailly Jacob,
Christelle Hirt.

Vivienne Westwood, Philip Treacy, Azzedine Alaia, Yoji Yamamoto,
Chantal Thomass, Jean-Paul Gaultier, Christian Dior, Comme des Garçons,
l'Opéra de Paris, Max, John Galliano, Véronique Leroy.

Laetitia Casta, Blanca Li, Mia Frye, Frédéric Beigbeder, Henri Salvador, Karen Park
Goude, Naomi Campbell, Hilton McConnico, Anna Piaggi, Sofie Nielander,
Rukmini Chaterjee, Natalia Semanova, Yulia Mizhuy, Lisa Pomares,
Leoni Van Amstel, Elma Regimbeau, Maria Malashenkova, Ellin J, Sasha Beznozyuk,
Ryanne Ten Haken, Mary Lee, Ana Paula Mizzetti, Paul Winston Goude,
Rossy de Palma, Jun Miyake.

Les studios de l'Olivier, Aléa films, Chromatix, Kashmir Films, RVZ, Janvier, RATP,
Pathé, Société d'exploitation de la tour Eiffel, Post Modern, Teletota,
L'affiche Européenne, Dahinden, Allarosa production, Flam & Co, Central Color,
Fauna & Films, Jacana, Women Management, Viva, IMG, Nathalie, Karin,
Sport Models, Marylin, Angels, Metropolitans, Next, Elite, Success, Teen.